Palmistry

FAMILY
MATTERS

Palmistry

LORI REID

WARD LOCK

A WARD LOCK BOOK

This edition published in the UK 1994
by Ward Lock
Villiers House
41/47 Strand
LONDON
WC2N 5JE

A Cassell Imprint

Distributed in the United States
by Sterling Publishing Co., Inc.
387 Park Avenue South, New York, NY 10016-8810

Distributed in Australia
by Capricorn Link (Australia) Pty Ltd
2/13 Carrington Road, Castle Hill NSW 2154

A British Library Cataloguing in Publication Data block for this
book may be obtained from the British Library

ISBN 0 7063 7323 5

Typeset by Columns of Reading Ltd
Printed and bound in Great Britain by Harper Collins

Contents

CONTENTS

THE MIRROR IN YOUR HANDS

'Look in the mirror and you will see a reflection of yourself. Look in your hands and you will see a mirror of your life.'

To an experienced hand reader your hands present a complete picture of you. Just as when you look in the mirror and see your image staring back at you, so your hands reflect back everything about you – how you think, how you feel, how you love, what you like or dislike, what state your health is in, whether you're a happy type or plain miserable, clever or barely scraping in at the bottom of the class, honest as the live-long day or occasionally not averse to being 'economical with the truth'.

Are you going to sail through life comfortably or will there be more downs than ups? Will you fall in love, marry, have children? And if so, how many? What sort of career path will you choose? What will you achieve in your life? Will you leave your mark, become rich or perhaps even famous?

The answers to these questions and many, many more can be found in your own hands.

WHAT'S WRITTEN IN YOUR HANDS

Most people are acquainted with palmistry – the art of

analysing the lines in the palm. But a true hand reading is, in fact, much wider than that because it considers the *whole* hand – fingers, nails, colour, temperature, fingerprints, mounts, lines – the lot.

For example, the shape of your hand tells a great deal about your character. There are four basic categories – Earth, Air, Fire and Water – into which each hand fits. If you possess an Earth hand, then straight away it reveals that you're a hard-worker, you're logical, rational, you have masses of common sense and your feet are very firmly on the ground. If your husband has a Water hand it means that he's dreamy, impressionable, sensitive, emotional and lives rather with his head in the clouds.

Already, with just this scant bit of information, you can start to build a picture of the type of people you and your husband are. And if, indeed, you do possess an Earth hand and he a Water one (or vice versa) then you've just got a pretty big hint that life together won't all be a bed of roses!

But don't be too downcast, however, because this is just the bottom line and there's masses more information to collect yet before drawing a final portrait of each other. And besides, differences of character make for interesting relationships.

Take a look at your fingers and compare their shape and length with those of your children. There are masses of tell-tale hints here about personality. Are your fingers, for instance, very long and those of your daughter very short? If that is the case, then her mind will be like quicksilver and when it comes to picking up any new skills, she'll leave you trailing in the dust. But, when it comes to close detailed work, you'll beat her hands down because you're the one with the patience and staying power to see the job through to the end. And then the nails, too, indicate a great deal about people's temperament. Does your new boyfriend have a wide oblong-shaped nail on his thumb? If so, watch out because this is a sign of a very quick volcanic temper!

It's a good idea, too, to familiarize yourself with your fingerprints because these will tell you about how you like to function in life. Loops show an absolute horror of a 9–to–5 boring routine type of job whilst whorls reveal a need, at all times, to be in charge or in control of the situation.

The way you think and feel, the way you love and relate to others, the sort of career best suited to you are all depicted in your lines. In fact, you'd be amazed at how much your lines can tell about you from the type of lover you are right down to when you're likely to move house or even break a leg.

Once you start reading people's hands you'll find yourself unlocking all sorts of skeletons from their cupboards. Keeping secrets from the experienced eye of a hand reader is very difficult to do!

But there's no doubt that the benefits of being able to interpret a hand are tremendous. A good reading will not only give you a vast insight into a person's character and personality, into his or her state of health or well-being, but it will also give valuable information about possible events which can alert that person to problems or opportunities that are likely to happen in the future.

And that's important because we all have choices and we can decide whether to go along blindly, stumbling from situation to situation, or to get some sort of idea of what's likely to be in store for us around the corner. If we have even the merest inkling of what might happen tomorrow, next week or even next year, then we can be prepared either to fend off any potentially unpleasant events or be alerted not to miss any good opportunities that may be winging their way in our direction.

LEFT OR RIGHT?

When it comes to reading the hand, many people are confused about which hand to look at, whether it should be their right or left one. Often you may have heard it said that 'the left is what you're born with and the right is what you make for yourself'. This is total hog-wash so, to put the record straight, here is the rule.

FOR RIGHT-HANDERS

Your right hand is known as the **DOMINANT HAND** and deals with the *external* you. That is, how you are, or how you behave in public, your active role in the outside world, events concerning your life, your loves, your job and career. In fact, anything to do with the picture you present to others and also how other people see you.

Your left hand is the **PASSIVE HAND** and this deals with the *private*, inner you. How you feel deep inside, how you respond instinctively, how you were as a child and how you are now when you let your hair down in the privacy of your own home. These are the areas of your life that are represented by your left hand.

FOR LEFT-HANDERS

Life in the past was tough on you left-handers and indeed, despite the fact that you are no longer forced to go against your nature and write with your right hand any more, you are in the minority and so things can still be fairly difficult for you. Pot handles, scissors, watch winders are all round the wrong way for you, and if you've ever experienced being taught to knit by one of the 'other lot', you'll know just how frustrating life can be in a world of right-handers. As if in *Alice Through the Looking Glass*, you live on the other side of the mirror to the rest of us.

But take heart, you make up something like 13 per cent of the population and if you watch Wimbledon you'll see just how many left-handers there are amongst the top seeds. In many sports, left-handers definitely seem to have the advantage.

When it comes to reading your hand, simply reverse the order for right-handers so that your left is your DOMINANT HAND and your right becomes your PASSIVE HAND.

FOR THE AMBIDEXTROUS

Are you truly ambidextrous? If so, you're going to be a problem – at least in terms of hand reading, that is. Somehow you have to find if, in fact, there is even the slightest dominance in either of your hands. Firstly, decide which hand you feel most comfortable writing with. The one that's happiest holding the pen and writing can be termed the DOMINANT HAND. If there's still some doubt, try this. Without thinking, pretend to brush your hair, or brush your teeth. The hand you would automatically raise to carry out these actions is your DOMINANT HAND, so read as for the right of the right-hander.

CHANGING LINES

Finally, it is important to remember that the lines in your hand can change. They can grow and develop or shrink and fade according to your life-style, your state of health, the decisions you make and your general attitude to life. So, if you don't like the look of something you see in your hand, you needn't necessarily be stuck with it. Reading our hands can help us to detect our faults so that we can put them right. But it can also bring to light our hidden assets, our gifts and talents, and encourage us to develop and then to make the best that we possibly can out of them.

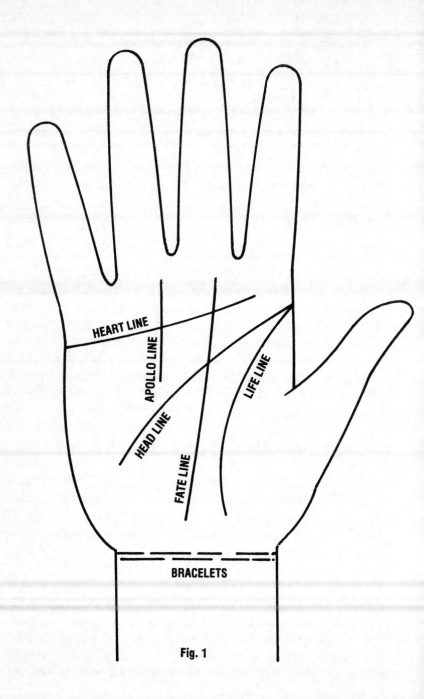

HEART LINE

APOLLO LINE

HEAD LINE

FATE LINE

LIFE LINE

BRACELETS

Fig. 1

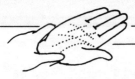

WATCH HOW THEY GROW

Have you ever stopped to have a really good look at the lines in your palm? If you have, you may have noticed how, from time to time, some of the markings seem to change. Indeed, many people are surprised to learn that their hands can and do change. Lines can grow longer, thicker, fatter. They can split, develop islands and even disappear altogether.

There are all sorts of reasons why your lines may change. A sudden emotional upset, for example, can imprint almost overnight some fine horizontal dashes across the tips of the fingers. With the lessening of the stress, these fine lines will simply fade away.

Ill-health can make its presence known in your hand years before a doctor might be able to diagnose it in the surgery. Certain types of chaining in the line could suggest that the body is out of salts. Islands in the life line, or a main line which becomes fuzzy may also point out that not all is as well as it might seem. But the strengthening of a line, the development of a branch or the appearance of a particular influence line are all early signs of better times ahead so that plans can be made in readiness of those events.

Because we have free will, it is possible for us to control many situations and events in our lives. The markings in our hands are laid down long before the events happen so an understanding of what they could mean is very useful in helping us plan ahead and in making important decisions which could influence the very course of our lives.

To keep one step ahead, then, it would be very useful for you to regularly take your own hand prints and those of your family so that you can keep a record of any changes that might occur. Birthdays are often a good time to take a print or perhaps the whole family can be done in one fell swoop, say, around Christmas or at the beginning of the new year.

TAKING HAND PRINTS

Taking a print can be rather a messy business but it can be good fun too. You can bet your bottom dollar, though, that just as you've inked your hands ready to put them on a sheet of paper, the phone will go or the front-door bell will ring or you'll suddenly need to scratch the tip of your nose or something – it always happens!

You'll have no trouble persuading your children to join in because they will think it's great fun to do and it's particularly interesting to keep a record of their hand prints as these will readily show the developing trends year by year.

The best ink to use is water-soluble lino printing ink. Make sure it is water-soluble then it will simpy wash off with soap and water. If it isn't, you'll need all sorts of solvents to get it off. If you can't get the ink there are several everyday household materials in your cupboards which will do the trick just as well. Lipstick or boot-polish, for example, will do very nicely, and you can experiment with anything else you think might work. The important thing to remember is not to apply it too thickly because this will just make a splodgy mess.

CHECK LIST FOR MAKING HAND PRINTS

▶ Lino printing ink (water-soluble), or a dark lipstick, or boot polish

▶ A printer's roller, or an empty wine or milk bottle

▶ A sheet of glass, or a formica board, or a piece of silver foil

▶ Paper (large enough to comfortably take an adult-sized hand)

▶ A table knife

▶ A sharp pencil or biro

▶ Tissues

▶ Towel

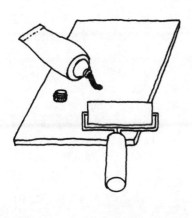

1. If using lino printing ink, squeeze about 1 cm (½ in) of the ink onto the glass/board/ silver foil. With the roller/bottle spread the ink evenly until it thinly covers the surface. Using the roller, roll the ink smoothly over the palm and fingers, making sure to cover a good 2–3 cm (¾–1 in) of the wrist.

2. If you are using lipstick or

tinned shoe polish, gently rub it all over the hand.

3. Next, fold the towel and place it on a table with a sheet of paper on top of it. Place the hand in your natural pose **AS COMFORTABLY AS POSSIBLE** on the paper.

4. Often you will find that the central part of the palm may not print so, next time, ink the hand again, place it on a fresh sheet of paper and then slip the knife underneath the paper and press up into the hollow part of the palm. You may have to repeat this procedure several times until you get a good print. Take several good prints of each hand.

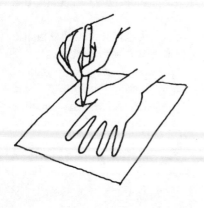

5. It's important to draw the outline of the hand on each print but it can be difficult over a spongy towel. Try if you can whilst taking the print, or else, after the hands have been washed and dried, the printed sheet of paper can be placed on a hard surface and the hand repositioned over the print so that the outline can be easily traced.

6. Finally, mark each sheet with the person's details:

- Date when print taken
- Name
- Sex
- Date of birth
- Right-/left-handed

The finished hand print should look like this:

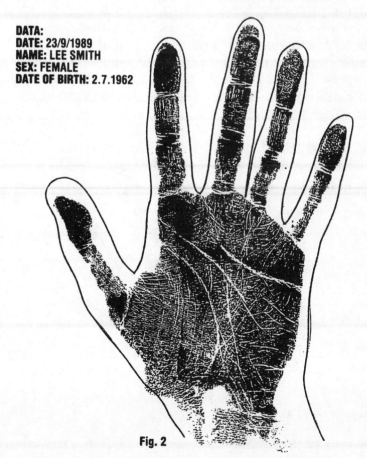

DATA:
DATE: 23/9/1989
NAME: LEE SMITH
SEX: FEMALE
DATE OF BIRTH: 2.7.1962

Fig. 2

Do this for each member of your family, friends or loved ones and you'll soon build up a record of their growth and development. You'll be able to see whether they're going through more or less stress than last time, whether any more success or movement lines are developing, whether any signs of ill-health are showing up, what sort of opportunities are in store for the coming year. You'll even be able to advise them about their school work or their jobs, about their relationships, finances and lots more.

If there's a new baby in the family, start to take his or her hand prints right from birth onwards and watch them growing year after year. A series of prints like this makes a fascinating collection and children love to compare their own hands with those when they were tiny. And besides, imagine what they'd be worth one day if that child became a really famous pop singer...

PRINTS OF A CHILD TAKEN

AT 1 YEAR

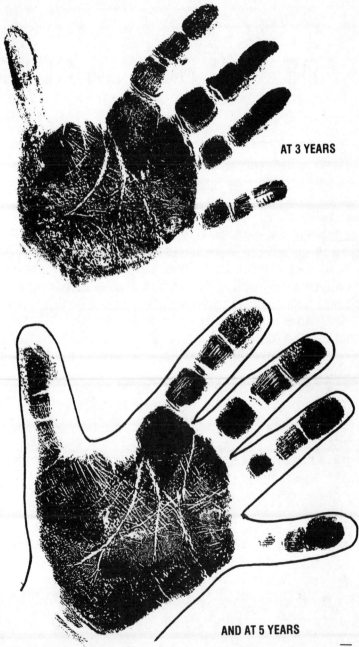

AT 3 YEARS

AND AT 5 YEARS

ARE YOU HOT OR COLD?

Have you ever noticed when you shake hands how some people have very hot hands whilst others are always icy cold? You may hear people saying 'Cold hands, warm heart', but in terms of hand reading it simply isn't true. Another saying, 'Warm hands, warm heart', is much more accurate.

In fact temperature, and colour for that matter too, can certainly tell a lot about a person's temperament and, very importantly, about his or her health as well. So next time someone holds out his hand to shake yours take note of its colour, whether it feels hot or cold, rough or smooth, whether it's 'limp-wristed' or grips you like a vice.

A word of warning, though. Before making any judgements about the temperature of someone's hand do be sure of your facts. Hot sweaty hands immediately after a strenuous session in an aerobics class isn't quite the same thing as hot sweaty hands at room temperature having sat immobile for the last half an hour.

★ **HOT HANDS**
- Hot hands indicate warmth and vitality. These people are positive, forthright and enthusiastic.
- Hot, very dry hands suggest a feverish condition whilst hot and sweaty ones often hint at an over-active thyroid.

★ COLD HANDS
- People with naturally cold hands have a tendency to be emotionally cool and calculating. Often they are critical and suspicious of others.
- If the hands are cold and dry it could be a sign of an under-active thyroid. But cold and clammy hands go with an anxious and nervous disposition. If you have ever had to deal with anyone who has just had an accident or received bad news you will know that their hands immediately go cold and clammy as this is one of the symptoms of shock.

★ RED HANDS
- Red hands show an intense, passionate nature. These people are usually over-active and generally hyped up. Impatience is another characteristic associated with red hands. Beware here a tendency to over-indulge.
- Very red hands often go with an aggressive, fighting spirit and a violent temper. These people are prone to high blood pressure.

★ WHITE HANDS
- White hands show a cool, impersonal type, someone who is uninspired and unenthusiastic about life. Lack of vitality and a poor circulation often go with very white hands.

★ BLUE HANDS
- Hands that are noticeably tinged with blue can denote a rather negative and pessimistic attitude to life. These people may suffer with circulatory problems and show a vulnerability to diseases of the heart.

★ YELLOW HANDS
- People with hands that are yellow or of a sallow

shade, (other than those that have been yellowed by a sun tan) usually have a morbid or jaundiced view of life. They tend to suffer with stomach or gastric conditions, or liver or gall bladder complaints.

★ **SMOOTH, SATIN SKIN**
- A fine, smooth, satiny skin highlights a sensitive, refined person. On the health front, though, these people may possibly be susceptible to rheumatism.

★ **ROUGH SKIN**
- Rough skin belongs to practical, down-to-earth, hard-working types. Because of their earthiness, they do tend to be somewhat unrefined and may lack sensitivity towards others.

★ **FIRM, ELASTIC HANDS**
- Firm, elastic hands that are springy to the touch indicate active, energetic people with a strong constitution and good health. They generally possess a happy nature too.

★ **HARD, INFLEXIBLE HANDS**
- Hard, inflexible hands immediately suggest someone who is over-controlled and tense with a fixed mentality and a rigid attitude of mind. Such people are prone to worry and anxiety.

★ **FLEXIBLE HANDS**
- Flexible hands and fingers denote an adaptable, open, easy-going person, someone who is easy to live with.

★ **SOFT HANDS**
- People with soft hands are gentle, sympathetic and sensitive. They are warm and loving types and always kind and helpful.

★ THICK, FLABBY HANDS

- Hands that are thick and flabby to the touch reveal a slow, lazy attitude. These people have a tendency to dream their way through life for they have good ideas but completely lack any motivation or drive to put those ideas into motion. They tend to be sensual and self-indulgent and like to pamper themselves a lot for they are strongly attracted to the dolce vita. Because of their preoccupation with themselves they tend to be totally insensitive to the needs of others.

★ THIN HANDS

- Hands that feel almost paper thin show a lack of stamina. People who possess this type of hand are usually physically weak types with low energy levels. They have a tendency to allow themselves to be swept along by other sturdier, more enthusiastic types.

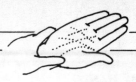

WHAT TYPE ARE YOU?

Take a good look around, when you're standing at the bus stop or waiting in the queue at the post office, at other people's hands. The more hands you look at, the more you'll start to notice the different shapes. Soon, you will become well versed in the art of spotting similarities. 'Aha,' you'll cry, 'that hand looks just like my Susan's/my doctor's/my next-door neighbour's!'

In fact, there's a good chance that you'd be right because there are just four basic types into which all our hands fit. These are called EARTH, AIR, FIRE and WATER. And if you think the shape of your friend's hand, or that of your husband or of your uncle, for that matter, looks very similar to that of your boss, then it's very likely that they will have certain characteristics or habits in common.

The basic hand shape denotes the fundamental character of an individual. Of course, each hand is unique – there are no two hands exactly the same as each other, not even those of identical twins. But the *shape* is the important fact. After that you have to take into account other information that you find out from the fingerprints, the nails and the lines on the palms. Each bit of information goes towards painting a clearer picture of the individual until finally you have painted a completely unique portrait of that person.

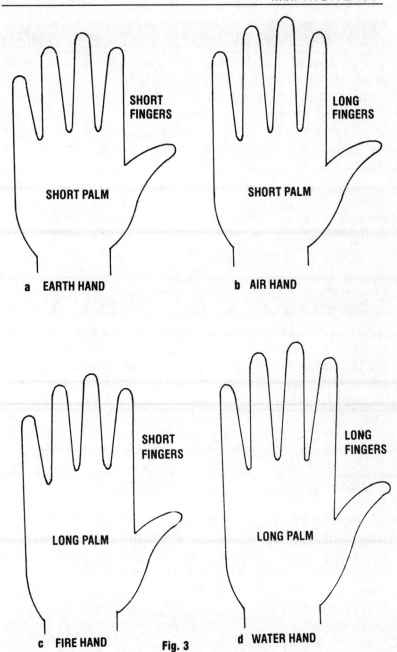

a EARTH HAND

b AIR HAND

c FIRE HAND   Fig. 3

d WATER HAND

FAMILY TREES

The shape of hands runs in families. You may have noticed that your son's hands look like yours whereas those of your daughter, perhaps, look like her father's. When you say to one of your offspring, 'You're just like your grandmother', or 'You remind me of your uncle so-and-so', it's highly likely that their hand shapes will match. Check it out and see.

An interesting little experiment is to simply draw around each person's hands and then to match up the outline shapes. Those who have similar shaped hands will have similar characters. Then you'll be able to run through all the current members of your family showing who has inherited their characters from whom.

HAND SHAPES

When it comes to actually deciding which of the four types a particular hand belongs to, it can get a little tricky. Some hands will fit perfectly into one or other of the categories and this will be known as a pure type. Others, however, may not quite match up a hundred per cent. Still others will be a combination, linking elements from two (or sometimes more) of the types. Here, you'll have to decide which type the hand is *most* like and then select the appropriate characteristics from the other categories. Have a go, the more you do the easier it gets.

The way to classify the hand shape is to look at the palms and fingers separately. The palm can be long and narrow giving it an oblong appearance or it can be short and square-looking. The fingers can either be short or they can be long. Short fingers aren't usually any longer than three-quarters the length of the palm. More than three-quarters the length of the palm or even longer, classifies them as long fingers.

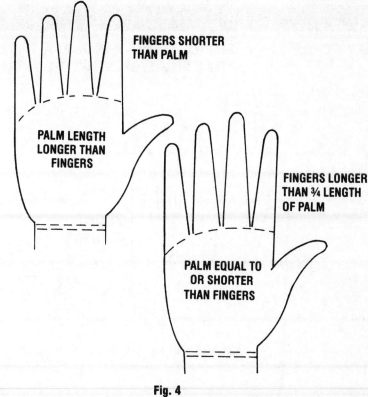

FINGERS SHORTER THAN PALM

PALM LENGTH LONGER THAN FINGERS

FINGERS LONGER THAN ¾ LENGTH OF PALM

PALM EQUAL TO OR SHORTER THAN FINGERS

Fig. 4

So, when the palm is short and the fingers, too, are short, you're looking at an EARTH hand. When the palm is short but the fingers are long, it's an AIR hand. If the palm is long but the fingers are short, then it's a FIRE hand. But if palm and fingers are both long, this is typically a WATER hand.

Listed below are the descriptions and characteristics for each type. But don't forget that at this stage they are very general – the bottom line of the reading – and all the other information you will glean through the book will slowly build up and modify the picture. Also, if the hand isn't a pure type, you will have to blend some of the descriptions together.

THE EARTH HAND

KEY WORDS: **SOLID, HARD-WORKING, PRACTICAL, DOWN-TO-EARTH**

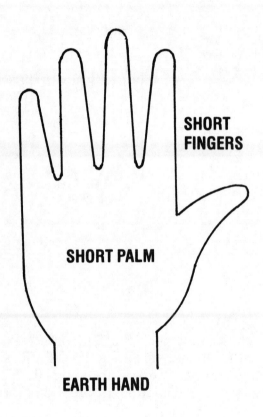

SHORT FINGERS

SHORT PALM

EARTH HAND

DESCRIPTION:

SHAPE	Square palm, short fingers
FINGERPRINTS	Arches or loops
LINES	Very few major lines

CHARACTER:

PERSONALITY   Earthy, down-to-earth, stolid sort of person

MENTALITY   Rational, logical, positive

EMOTIONS   Stable, solid as a rock, uncomplicated, undemonstrative

WORK   Hard-working, practical, methodical worker, needs routine, dislikes change, loves the outdoors, hates being cooped up in an office, enjoys working with hands

HOBBIES   Gardening, nature rambles, d.i.y., handicrafts

POLITICS   Strong believer in law and order: Conservative, right-wing, reactionary

SUITABLE OCCUPATIONS: Farmer, gardener, game-keeper, policeman, soldier, mechanic, engineer, baker, banker, economist, carpenter, decorator, HGV driver, plant machinery operator, accountant, doctor, vet, geographer, geologist, miner, teacher, lawyer, barrister, judge, technician

THE AIR HAND

KEY WORDS: **FULL OF LIFE, CHATTY, EXCITABLE, CURIOUS**

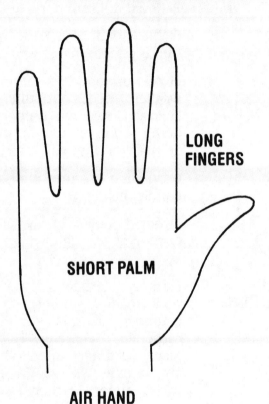

LONG FINGERS

SHORT PALM

AIR HAND

DESCRIPTION:

SHAPE	Short palm, long fingers
FINGERPRINTS	Loops
LINES	Well-formed, well-constructed, clear lines

CHARACTER:

PERSONALITY

Great talker and a good communicator, enjoys company of others, cheerful, chatty, bird-like, interested in everything around them, flexible and adaptable

MENTALITY

Inquisitive, buzzing mentality, quick learner, mercurial mind, wants to know how things fit and go together, eternal student

EMOTIONS

Fairly well-balanced, well-controlled can be cool

WORK

Work must be stimulating, hates boring 9-to-5, needs variety and change, anything investigative

HOBBIES

Travelling, reading, T.V., cinema, debating, writing

POLITICS

Loves rhetoric, political debate, party politics:
Liberal, socialist, democrat

SUITABLE OCCUPATIONS:

Detective, investigator, private eye, researcher, student, teacher, lecturer, travel agent, guide, airline hostess, pilot, representative, journalist, writer, radio broadcaster, T.V. presenter, artist, editor, publisher, orator, communications, after-dinner speaker, consultant, estate agent, salesman, hotelier, dancer, photographer, public relations

THE FIRE HAND

KEY WORDS: **EXTROVERT, BUSY, ENTHU-
SIASTIC, ENERGETIC**

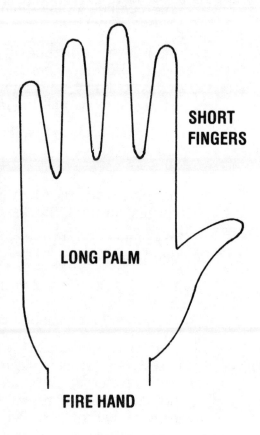

**SHORT
FINGERS**

LONG PALM

FIRE HAND

DESCRIPTION:

SHAPE	Long palms, short fingers
FINGERPRINTS	Mainly whorls
LINES	Many lines but strong and well-formed

CHARACTER:

PERSONALITY — Fun-loving, happy-go-lucky type, enthusiastic, strong, forthright, bustling personality, inspires and influences others, boundless energy, uninhibited, show-off

MENTALITY — Bright, intelligent, alert

EMOTIONS — Excitable, emotional, volatile, flashes of temper

WORK — Helpful to others, always on the go, likes to be in charge, good organizer, ability to inspire and motivate others, positive attitude, strong qualities of leadership, ability to cope with stressful situations

HOBBIES — All sports, dancing, voluntary work, crafts

POLITICS — Politics that inspire and fire the imagination:
Monarchist, Republican, revolutionary

SUITABLE OCCUPATIONS: — Business, manager, organizer, entrepreneur, lecturer, sportsman or woman, designer, dealer, stockbroker, missionary, politician, member of the clergy, fireman/woman, writer, craftsman, engineer, project manager, astronaut, social worker, artist, sculptor, healer

THE WATER HAND

KEY WORDS: **EMOTIONAL, IMPRESSIONABLE, SENSITIVE, ARTISTIC**

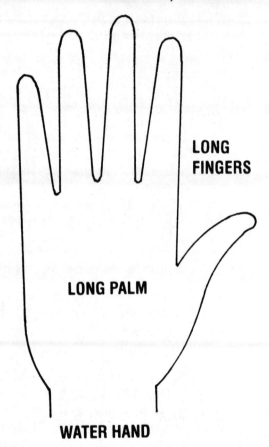

LONG FINGERS

LONG PALM

WATER HAND

DESCRIPTION:

SHAPE	Long palms, long fingers
FINGERPRINTS	Loops
LINES	Many fine lines, often resembling a spider's web

CHARACTER:

PERSONALITY — Gentle, sensitive, caring people, cultured, urbane, refined, good taste, passive, easily influenced, tendency to live with head in the clouds

MENTALITY — Quiet, thoughtful, contemplative

EMOTIONS — Highly sensitive, emotions over-rule reason, moody, sulky

WORK — Needs a peaceful, unstressed working environment, cannot cope with pressure, impractical but very good with fine detailed work, painstaking with precision and minutiae, easily bored

HOBBIES — Occult subjects, painting, sketching, museums, art galleries, music

POLITICS — Humanitarian, green, liberal, socialist

SUITABLE OCCUPATIONS: — Artist, poet, fashion designer, model, position in the fashion industry, the glamour business, psychic, musician, a post in retailing, shopkeeper, clerical/office worker, actor, the monastic or contemplative life, market research, astrologer, social worker, healer, watchmaker, tailor, beauty therapist, psychologist, interior designer, nurse, doctor

LUMPS AND BUMPS

Hold out your hand and look closely at all the little fleshy lumps and bumps that make up your palm. These are known as mounts and some, you will notice, are bigger than others. Some are high, some are flat, others are springy or hard. Whatever they look like, the shape or appearance of these mounts is very important when it comes to reading a hand because each one will reveal certain qualities about the individual.

Now take an even closer look at each mount. Inspect it well and decide what sort of markings you can see on it. Perhaps you can make out a square shape, perhaps a triangle or possibly even a star. Markings on the mounts have specific meanings. Sometimes they reveal special talents, they may stand as warnings, show protection or denote brilliant potential.

There are eight mounts in all, as shown in the illustration. Starting from below the index finger and working across the top they are called the mounts of Jupiter, Saturn, Apollo and Mercury. On the outside edge, and below the Mount of Mercury, there is the Mount of Upper Mars. Then, working across the base of the palm just above the wrist you will find the Mount of Luna on the outside edge, whilst on the other side the large area around the base of the thumb is the Mount of Venus. Immediately above the Mount of Venus, and completing the circle around the palm is the Mount of Lower Mars. All these mounts surround a flat area in the

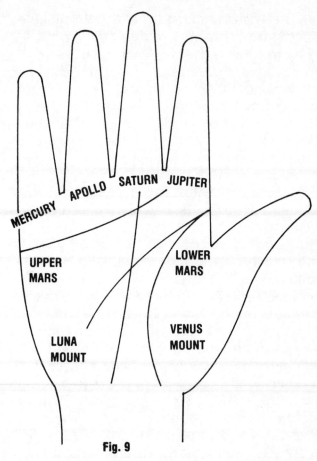

Fig. 9

centre of the palm which is known as the Plain of Mars.

Although on most hands the Venus area will look like the largest and most padded of all the mounts, it is important to notice which mount you would consider the dominant one. Usually this is the one which looks odd or disproportionate against the others. For example, take a hand where all the little fleshy pads seem fairly flattened and then you notice that Mercury, let's say, rises to a little peak, rather like a tiny hill. Mercury, then, in this case is the dominant mount.

Because each mount reflects certain qualities, if one particular area is huge it shows that the owner of that hand is strong in those particular qualities. If the mount is non-existent then he or she will lack the qualities represented by it. When a mount is dominant, then it means that that person will be characterized by those qualities. So, people with dominant Mercury mounts will be instantly recognized as chatty, curious and witty, they are quick to learn and have a ready word for every situation. But, if all the mounts seem to be equal, there may not be any dominant characteristics that especially stand out, so that person would be considered fairly well-balanced.

With a bit of practice, and by looking at the hands of your family and friends, you'll soon be able to spot the differences in the sizes and shapes of the mounts. Remember that the Venus Mount will usually be the biggest area but don't let that confuse you into thinking that everybody you see will be Venus dominant. If it truly does swamp the hand then you would be right but generally try to consider the others in comparison to each other.

The more hands you look at the more you will notice the different markings on the mounts. There are several sorts of lines and patterns to look out for. Sometimes you may see a single horizontal or vertical line running across a mount, or perhaps a little group of lines together. The types of patterns to watch for are stars, squares, crosses, grilles or triangles, as illustrated on pages 41–53. Triangles suggest success, squares offer protection, crosses and grilles are generally unfavourable and stars have a double meaning – in some areas they show great promise whilst in others they can mean misfortune.

Some people, you will find, have very few markings on their mounts whilst other people's mounts will be covered in all sorts of lines. If there is a dominant

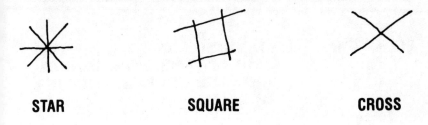

STAR   **SQUARE**   **CROSS**

GRILLE   **TRIANGLE**

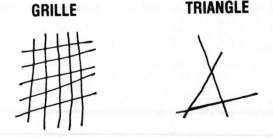

Fig. 10

mount it will usually be that one that has some pretty obvious marks on it.

When you are examining the mounts you may come across different types of patterns that will not be covered here at this stage. That's because there are some special formations on certain areas that have very specific meanings and which generally refer to talents and career. If the marking isn't mentioned here check it out in **Special Markings** on page 116.

THE MOUNT OF JUPITER

KEY WORDS: **STANDING IN LIFE, SELF-RESPECT, AMBITION, LEADERSHIP, THE CHURCH, POLITICS, THE LAW**

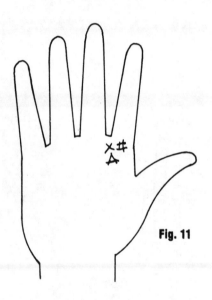

Fig. 11

LOCATION   The mount of Jupiter is located just beneath the index finger, as shown

QUALITIES   Confidence, optimism, generosity. Warmth and friendliness. Good at command and at taking charge. Good-natured. Religion important in life and often attracted to the church. Found in the armed forces. Strong ideas about politics, society and the environment. Honest.

Proud. Loves living life to the full. A *bon viveur*. Huge appetite.

SHAPE

Under-developed: Lack of confidence, lazy, selfish, lack of self-respect, inferiority complex

Over-developed: Self-indulgence, wastefulness, haughtiness, conceit, extravagance, greed, bossiness, domineering

Dominant: Will strongly display the qualities associated with this mount

MARKINGS

Square: Protection of one's standing in life

Star: Happiness and success in career

Cross: Good relationship

Triangle: General good luck

Grille: Bossiness and power-seeking

DESCRIPTION OF TYPE:

Medium build but strong and virile. Generally muscular but inclined to over-weight in later years. Good complexion, smooth skin, full mouth, large white teeth, large eyes, straight nose. Brown or reddish-coloured hair.

HEALTH PROBLEMS:

Tendency to put on weight and become obese. Digestive problems. Prone to fevers, gout and stroke.

THE MOUNT OF SATURN

KEY WORDS: **SERIOUSNESS, RESPONSIBILITY, STUDY, CONTEMPLATION, DUTY, HARD WORK**

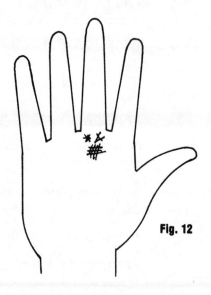

Fig. 12

LOCATION

The mount of Saturn is located beneath the middle finger, as shown

QUALITIES

This mount is the one exception to the rule as it's far better for it to be flat, under-developed or non-existent for best effect. Qualities associated with this area include: common sense, patience, solitude, melancholy, over-cautious, seriousness, sobriety. Love of study and research. Stability, pessimism. A love and understanding of animals and a magnetic attraction to the land. Interests in real estate and property. Strong musical talents.

SHAPE

Under-developed: Not as gloomy, moody or pessimistic as the qualities suggest

Over-developed: Miserable, critical, cold personality, morbid, selfish, cynical, reclusive, miserly, suspicious, bitter, paranoid

Dominant: Read as for the over-developed mount

MARKINGS

Square: Protection in career and finances

Star: Accident-prone

Cross: A sudden death

Triangle: Excellent in research, interests in scientific subjects

Grille: Depression

DESCRIPTION OF TYPE:

Tall, thin and gaunt. Sallow complexion. Long, thin face, high bony cheek bones, small eyes, often deep-set, long nose, thin mouth. Straight dark hair inclined to lankiness. Tendency to stoop.

HEALTH PROBLEMS:

Disorders of the nervous system. Poor bones and teeth, often losing teeth early in life. Prone to rheumatism, tumours, cancer, paralysis.

THE MOUNT OF APOLLO

KEY WORDS: **THE ARTS, CREATIVITY, HAPPI-
NESS, LUCK, A SUNNY DISPOSI-
TION**

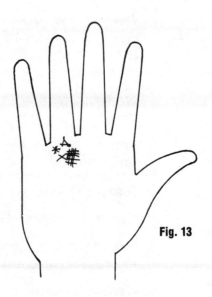

Fig. 13

LOCATION

The mount of Apollo, also called the mount of Sun, is found beneath the ring finger, as shown

QUALITIES

A love of all creative and artistic subjects – painting, writing, music, etc. Refinement, intelligence, appreciation of beauty, a need to be surrounded by beautiful things. Contentment and self-fulfillment. Enthusiasm and optimism. Inventiveness and intuition.

SHAPE	***Under-developed:*** Lack of interest in culture and the arts
	Over-developed: Vanity, ostentation. A poseur. Pretentiousness, boastfulness, snobbishness. A desire for fame
	Dominant: Will display the qualities associated with this mount
MARKINGS	***Square:*** Protection against scandal
	Star: Wealth and success
	Cross: Financial loss, failed ambitions
	Triangle: Exceptionally good sign denoting luck, success and fame
	Grille: Vanity
DESCRIPTION OF TYPE:	Usually good-looking with a flowing abundance of golden or rich brown hair. Pink and white complexion with well-proportioned features, even mouth and sparkling eyes. Graceful in movement and rather athletic.
HEALTH PROBLEMS:	Spinal problems. Poor sight. Heart disease.

THE MOUNT OF MERCURY

KEY WORDS: **ARTICULACY, WIT, QUICK-SILVER MENTALITY, FAST-MOVING, INTELLIGENCE, SHREWDNESS**

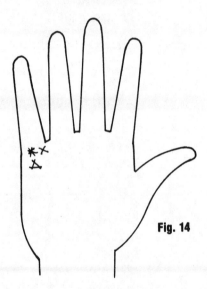

Fig. 14

LOCATION   The Mount of Mercury is found directly beneath the little finger, as shown

QUALITIES   Persuasiveness, silver-tongued, charm, ability to talk the hind leg off a donkey. Clever and astute. Need for change and variety in their lives. Liveliness and activity. Enjoyment of all forms of mental games, quizzes, cross-words, card games. Strong interests in travel, communications and the media.

SHAPE	**Under-developed:** No sense of humour, boring
	Over-developed: Schemer, prone to lying and cheating, excessive gift of the gab, lack of scruples, con-man, criminal tendencies
	Dominant: Will display the qualities associated with this mount
MARKINGS	**Square:** Protection against brain fatigue
	Star: Success in business, in science, technology, in the media, in literature and all forms of study
	Cross: A prey to deception and trickery
	Triangle: Personal satisfaction in business and intellectual work
	Grille: Dishonest nature
DESCRIPTION OF TYPE:	Thin and often of average height, Peter-Pan quality which keeps them looking young. High forehead with quick, expressive eyes that don't miss a trick. Good clear voice.
HEALTH PROBLEMS:	Coughs, biliousness, speech impediments, nervous and mental disorders.

THE MOUNTS OF MARS

KEY WORDS: **MORAL OR PHYSICAL COURAGE, STRENGTH, DETERMINATION, ENDURANCE, TRUE GRIT, PASSION, INTENSITY**

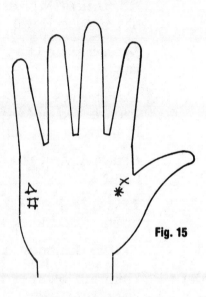

Fig. 15

LOCATION | There are two mounts of Mars. The Mount of Upper Mars (Mars passive) is found beneath the Mercury mount and that of Lower Mars (Mars active) lies beneath the Mount of Jupiter

QUALITIES | Upper Mars = moral courage, self-control, moral strength and fibre, fortitude.
Lower Mars = energy, activity, physical courage. Cool head in a crisis. Bravery.

SHAPE

Under-developed: Lack of courage, cowardice, lack of resistance, weakness

Over-developed: Rashness, aggressiveness, bullying, violence, sarcasm, abuse, mental or physical cruelty, pig-headedness

Dominant: Will display the qualities associated with these mounts

MARKINGS

Square: Protection in dangerous situations

Star: Success, achievements and honours in either a military career or from standing up to one's enemies

Cross: Enemies, accidents and physical danger

Triangle: Distinguished military career

Grille: Beware of accidents

DESCRIPTION OF TYPE:

Medium build, strong and stocky. Ruddy complexion, strong aquiline nose with wide nostrils. Big eyes.

HEALTH PROBLEMS:

Sore throats, circulatory problems, burns, fevers, accidents involving sharp objects.

THE MOUNT OF LUNA

KEY WORDS: **SENSITIVITY, RECEPTIVITY, IMAGINATION, ROMANCE**

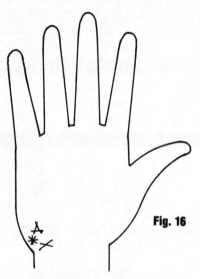

Fig. 16

LOCATION

The Mount of Luna is found at the base of the palm on the opposite side to the thumb and lying just above the wrist. A well-developed mount is recognised not only by its fullness, height and expanse across the hand but also by the marked curve it creates to the outside edge of the palm, as shown

QUALITIES

Romanticism, sensitivity to beauty and the seasons. Gentleness. Creativity, imaginative. Ability to write, paint, compose poetry. Music lover. Earth Mother. Intuitive, psychic. Affinity to water.

SHAPE

Under-developed: Unsympathetic, unimaginative, hypochondria, superstitious

Over-developed: Silliness, flightiness, eccentricity, over-sensitivity, touchy, moody, melancholic, hysterical, changeable, indecisive, lack of common sense, dreamy, unrealistic, mentally restless

Dominant: Will display the qualities associated with this mount

MARKINGS

Square: Protection against accidents whilst travelling

Star: Brilliant imagination. Beware danger at sea

Cross: Beware danger travelling and at sea

Triangle: Success in the creative fields

Grille: Moodiness, highly-strung, possible gynaecological problems

DESCRIPTION OF TYPE:

Tall and muscular. Very pale complexion and generally soft, fine and light-coloured hair. Eyes are large and round. Hands are plump and soft.

HEALTH PROBLEMS:

Problems of the stomach and the urinary tract. Rheumatism, gout, bronchial disorders. Mental health problems — (as in 'lunacy' which comes from the word Luna).

THE MOUNT OF VENUS

KEY WORDS: **HAPPY, VIRILE, HEALTHY, SEXY, ALIVE, ENTHUSIASTIC**

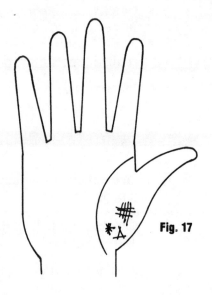

Fig. 17

LOCATION

The Mount of Venus is located on the palm beneath the thumb and is often known as the 'ball of the thumb', as shown

QUALITIES

Sensuality, excitability, vitality, attractiveness. Warm-heartedness, compassion, love, friendliness, optimism. Strong constitution. Pursuit of pleasure. Musical. Happy, *joie de vivre*, generosity, honesty, truthfulness. Sexiness. Love of children.

SHAPE	***Under-developed:*** Cold, selfish, stand-offish, aloof. Physically delicate
	Over-developed: Sensuality, consuming passions, possessiveness, fickleness, easily infatuated
	Dominant: Will display the qualities associated with this mount
MARKINGS	***Square:*** Protection against emotional unhappiness, bad influences or treacherous attachments
	Star: Sex-appeal, emotional happiness
	Cross: A strong love in your life
	Triangle: Marriage brings power and position
	Grille: Emotional entanglements, possible gynaecological problems
DESCRIPTION OF TYPE:	Graceful and soft. Pink and white complexion, large brown eyes with long curling lashes, red lips, white teeth and healthy-looking pink gums. Delicate shell-like ears. Podgy, dimpled hands.
HEALTH PROBLEMS:	Generally healthy and quickly able to shake off any physical or psychological upsets. If any problems at all, they would be associated with the neck, throat and reproductive organs.

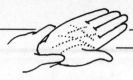

FINGERS AND THUMBS

Can you imagine how you would tie a shoe lace, peel a grape, do up your buttons, hold a pen, unscrew a bottle, cut with scissors, hold hands, use tools and generally get through a whole day's work, let alone a life time, without fingers and thumbs. Try it – just for a few minutes – frustrating, isn't it?

Sure, we would try to compensate by using other parts of our bodies. Our first line of attack, I suppose, would be to use our mouths and our teeth. And of course, we could always train our feet and our toes as substitutes. But it would all take so long, and it's so awkward and difficult, anyway. Thank goodness for fingers and thumbs!

When you stop to think about the hand in this way you start to realize just what a marvellous bit of engineering it is. Fingers and thumbs work together in a pincer movement so that we can hold and grip and pick things up – even the tiniest grain of sand. And it's our thumbs we have to thank for much of that ability. In fact, even when it comes to hand reading, our thumbs are the most important of all the digits.

THE THUMB

The thumb is made up of three sections, (see Fig. **18**). The top, or nail section, will tell you about your will power. The second part reflects your powers of reason.

The third section is the mount of Venus which has already been dealt with in the previous chapter.

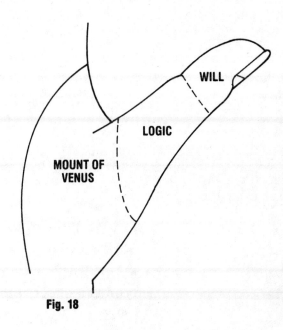

Fig. 18

When you're reading a thumb there are several points to take into consideration. Firstly you must measure the top two sections because their respective length is important. Next look at the tip. It might be sharp and pointed; it might have a blunt square top; some are pleasantly rounded, whilst others are like spatulas. Occasionally, you may come across an unusual type that's known as a clubbed thumb.

Hold the thumb and wiggle it about a bit. Does it bend easily at the top joint so that it's flexible or is there

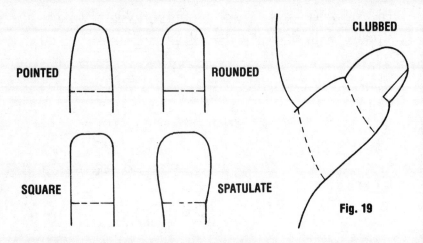

POINTED ROUNDED

CLUBBED

SQUARE SPATULATE

Fig. 19

no give in it whatsoever? And how far will it open out from the palm? All these factors will give vital information about the person.

KEY WORDS:	**WILL POWER, DETERMINATION, REASON, LOGIC**
MEANING	***Top section:*** Strength of will, determination, persistence, strength of character.
	Second section: Powers of reason, logic.
LENGTH	***Long:*** A thumb is long when it reaches half-way up the index finger. Long thumbs show elegance of mind, a go-ahead personality.
	Short: A thumb is short when it fails to reach half-way up the index. Very short thumbs denote a narrow mind and lack of intelligence.

Top section: If longer than the second section then strong-minded and determined. If very long, bossy, obstinate and unreasonable. If short, lack of willpower. If equal to second then well-balanced personality.

Second section: If longer than the top section shows uncertainty and indecision. If short, poor logical powers. If 'waisted' or narrow it shows tact and diplomacy.

TIP   ***Pointed:*** Scatters energies too easily, nervous type

Rounded: Impressionable, easily influenced

Square: Hard working

Spatulate: Also known as the potter's thumb, indicates practicality

Clubbed: Obstinate, unruly temper, coarse nature, violent

SUPPLENESS   ***Supple:*** Flexible, easy-going

Stiff: Inflexible, rigid attitudes

OPENING   ***Narrow angle:*** Closed, difficulty in adapting to new situations

Wide angle: Open, generous, gregarious, happy-go-lucky, easily swayed. If very wide, extravagant

THE FINGERS

The fingers are also known by classical names, as shown. The index is called Jupiter, the second is Saturn, the ring finger is Apollo and the little finger is known as Mercury. Each finger tells us something about a particular aspect of life and the sort of information we can get about a person will very much depend on the size and shape of his or her fingers and whether any are bent or crooked or whatever.

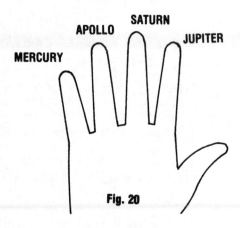

Fig. 20

Like the thumb they are made up of three sections. The top, or nail section, deals with our mental attitudes, the middle section with our practical abilities and the bottom section with material needs.

People with long fingers behave differently to those with short ones. To work out whether your fingers are long or short you first measure your middle finger and then your palm from the 'bracelet', where it meets the wrist, up to where it joins the middle finger. If your middle finger is any more than three-quarters the length of the palm you have long fingers. Any less, you can say your fingers are short.

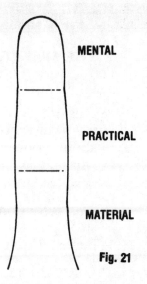

MENTAL

PRACTICAL

MATERIAL

Fig. 21

LONG FINGERS

People with long fingers are patient and slow. They have a keen eye for detail whether at home, in their work or about their own person. They tend to fiddle and fuss over trivial things. But, if you have a job which needs a meticulous mind and a careful hand, go for people with long fingers every time.

SHORT FINGERS

People with short fingers are quick but impatient. Often inspired, they pick things up quickly and are good at reading between the lines. They dislike finicky detail and prefer to take an overall view of everything. They make excellent planners and organizers but if you need someone to cross the t's and dot the i's, the short-fingered person is not for you.

THE INDEX FINGER

KEY WORDS

NAME

MEANING

LENGTH

STANCE

SECTIONS

THE SELF, THE EGO

Jupiter.

This finger represents your standing in life and reveals how you feel about yourself in the world and what you think about other people's impression of you.

Average: Confident, upright, a strong sense of justice and of personal honour.

Long: If long in comparison to the second finger then you love being in control, in charge, in command. Possibly a domineering nature.

Short: If very short, you have an inferiority complex probably due to a large chip on your shoulder.

Leaning away from all the other fingers shows ambition and an independent thinker.
Leaning towards the middle finger reveals a shy, retiring nature, a dislike of the limelight.

Top: When this section is long it tells of a spiritual mind. Thoughts turn to religion and 'higher things'.

Middle: If this section is long it shows executive ability, as well as a need to obtain and excel in material goods and wealth. When short, lack of managerial potential.

Bottom: If this part is long it shows pride and a need to rule.
If you have this section full and rounded it's a sign that you would excel in anything to do with catering. Good cooks, chefs and people who run restaurants often have a 'podgy' bottom section in this finger.

THE MIDDLE FINGER

KEY WORDS:	**DUTY, CAREFULNESS, SERIOUSNESS, MOODINESS**
NAME	Saturn.
MEANING	This finger represents anything to do with the basic needs of life. Agriculture, farming, mining or anything to do with the land. It's also associated with seriousness, with brooding and melancholy moods.
LENGTH	**Average:** An average length here, a finger which doesn't look either too long or too short in comparison to the rest, shows a person with a sense of duty who understands the meaning of responsibility.

Long: If this finger is very long in comparison to the others it shows a gloomy, morbid nature, someone who pours cold water over everything. In other words, a real wet blanket.

Short: Unconventional and often irresponsible.

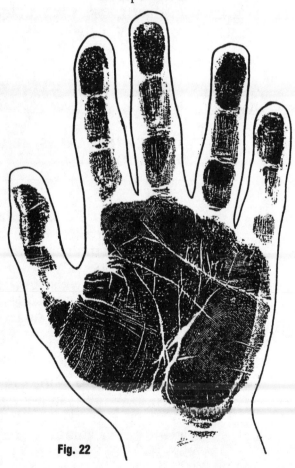

Fig. 22

STANCE

Leaning towards the index finger shows someone who is ambitious and enjoys the cut and thrust of a career. If you have this formation you may often feel a conflict between your duty to your home and children as opposed to your duty to your work.

Leaning towards the ring finger reveals a need for security. For you, your home is your nest and the centre of your universe.

SECTIONS

Top: When this section is long it tells of a serious nature. If any of your children have this you should encourage them to take up academic research because this is one of the signs of a love of study.

Middle: If this section of your hand is very long then you're a brilliant house-keeper. You're careful and cautious and when it comes to budgeting and monitoring your finances, you've got your finger right on the button! A long section here also shows green fingers and a love of gardening, farming, mining or anything to do with the land.

Bottom: If you know anyone who's rather mean and tight-fisted try to sneak a look at the bottom section of his middle finger – bet you it'll be very, very long!

THE RING FINGER

KEY WORDS:	**ART, CREATIVITY, CONTENTMENT**
NAME	Apollo.
MEANING	This finger deals with your sense of happiness and self-fulfilment. It reflects both artistic taste and creative talent.
LENGTH	***Average:*** A normal ring finger should be roughly the same length as the index finger. Average length shows a fair creative sense and style.

Long: A long ring finger tells that you live in a bit of a fantasy world, wanting to be surrounded by wealth and riches beyond your wildest dreams. Watch your finances if you fall for a person with a very long ring finger as this is also the sign of the gambler.

Short: A short finger here would show you're a bit of a philistine with no real appreciation for art or literature.

STANCE	Leaning towards the middle finger shows a need for security. Leaning towards the little finger, so that it creates a big gap between itself and the middle finger, shows someone who is resourceful. These are possibly shy people or anti-

social types who like their own company.

SECTIONS

Top: A long top section here shows great appreciation of art and literature.

Middle: When long this also shows a love of art.

Bottom: If this one is very long it's a tell-tale hint of vanity. Someone who has this feature would be very showy and ostentatious, with a lack of good taste. If this section is podgy, it's known as the 'collector's urge' and shows either a love of collecting things or simply a hoarding instinct.

THE LITTLE FINGER

KEY WORDS:

COMMUNICATIONS, WIT, BUSINESS, SCIENCE, LITERATURE

NAME

Mercury.

MEANING

The littlest finger of the hand has the widest range. It reflects our ability to talk, to reason, and to persuade others. It deals with business, with science, with literature, with communications and with the media.

LENGTH

Average: Well-balanced mentality, good powers of expression and good at business.

Long: If long, witty and articulate, good at speaking. Someone with a very long little finger has the ability to 'charm the birds off the trees', and is not averse to a little deception in order to get what he or she wants.

Short: If you have a very short little finger you may have some difficulty in expressing your thoughts in words.

STANCE

Leaning towards the ring finger reveals a clinging, dependent nature. Leaning away is an instantly recognized sign of a very independent spirit, someone who needs freedom to come and go, who can't bear to be restricted, hemmed in or cut off.

SECTIONS

Top: If this section is long it shows intelligence and a good head for scientific or academic work.

Middle: A long section here tells of a shrewd mind with plenty of common-sense. A sign of a clever person with plenty of imagination and a lively mentality.

Bottom: A long section means good communicative ability. But if very short it can suggest sexual inadequacy.

NAILS AND FINGERPRINTS

If the shape and size of our fingers give important clues about our personality, you'd be surprized to find how much more we can learn just from a close-up inspection of the very tips of our fingers.

On one side we have nails. You can manicure or paint them as much as you like but the basic shape of the nail will still sneak out all sorts of information that you may not be aware of.

On the other side we have fingerprints. Now, it doesn't take a Sherlock Holmes buff to remind us that if, perish the thought, we had in mind to do over the bank on the corner and we were stupid enough to leave our dabs all over the safe door that, very soon, they would find out who done it!

It's as plain to us all as the noses on our faces that our fingerprints are our personal identification marks. No two people have exactly the same prints. But what may not be quite so plain is that although fingerprints stand as our personal signatures, to those people who know what they mean, they can tell us an awful lot about our characters too.

THE NAILS

When we look at the nails it will be the actual shape of the living part that we must take into consideration, that is, the pink bit. However, apart from the shape, the actual condition of the nails themselves will give a lot away about their owners.

For example, nails which are badly chewed often point to an anxious type of person. Those that are beautifully manicured may suggest someone who thinks that appearance is very important and will take a lot of time and trouble about his or her personal grooming. Brittle, flaking nails may hint at a mineral imbalance.

So, when you're looking at nails make a mental note of everything you see – the size, the moons, the shape, the condition, and the colour.

COLOUR
Pink: Warm, even temper. Good health.

Red: Fiery, angry temper. Impulsive. Health prone to suffer from conditions associated with stressed circulation.

Blue: Cold extremities and poor circulation.

Yellow: Bilious type. Associated with jaundice or liver problems.

White: Cold, selfish, and cynical person. Health suffers from a lack of vitality.

Fig. 23

SIZE   ***Large:*** Easy-going, calm, steady nature. Good business sense. Good judgement.

Small: Active, energetic. Intuitive. Critical.

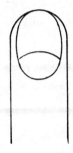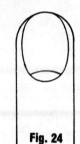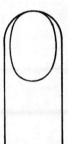

Fig. 24

MOONS   ***Large:*** Strong heart. Good circulation.

Small: Small, even moons show good health.

No moons: Poor circulation.

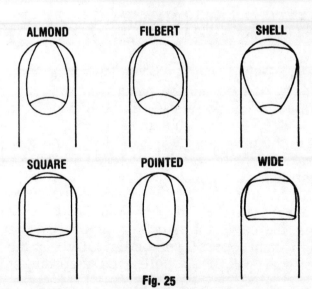

ALMOND   FILBERT   SHELL

SQUARE   POINTED   WIDE

Fig. 25

SHAPE

Almond: Gentle, refined, dreaming, sensitive.

Filbert: Romantic, nervy, possibly sulky.

Shell: Shell or fan-shaped nails indicate a nervous, highly-strung person.

Square: Solid, sensible, slow to anger.

Pointed: Very thin, pointed nails show a selfish, grasping personality. Neurotic type.

Wide: An oblong-shaped nail, broader than it is high, can sometimes be found on the thumb. It indicates sudden flashes of temper.

FINGERPRINTS

You will need to stand at a window or under a good light to be able to see the pattern on your finger tips clearly and even then it can still be difficult at the first attempt. Keep looking, though, and soon your eyes will adjust to the tiny squiggles, to the loops and the spirals that make up the fingerprints so readily understood and recognized by the police.

There are several different patterns of which you may have ten exactly the same on your hands or perhaps you may have a mixture – two or three whorls, say, and seven or eight loops. If you have a full set of the same pattern you will be a pure type according to the description given. If, though, you have a mixture of patterns you will display some of the qualities of one type and some qualities of the other.

Did you know that fingerprints can be inherited within the family? Spotting who has inherited what from whom can make a good family game. So check out which patterns you have and then compare them with those of your brothers and sisters or of your children. You may be surprised to find that your son, say, has exactly the same prints as you and that your daughter has the same as her father. Even stranger is when you find that one of your children has exactly the same patterns as you on one hand but those of your husband's on the other!

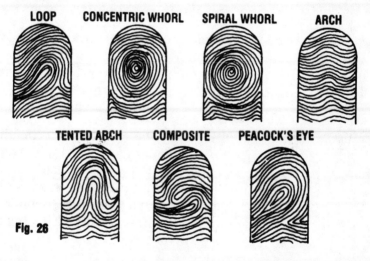

LOOP **CONCENTRIC WHORL** **SPIRAL WHORL** **ARCH**

TENTED ARCH **COMPOSITE** **PEACOCK'S EYE**

Fig. 26

LOOPS

Flexible, adaptable, versatile. Enjoys lots of interests and activities. Needs a busy, active life with plenty of stimulation. Creative. Good working with people. Loves the buzziness of communications and the media.

WHORLS

Deep, quiet type. Needs to be in charge and in control. Rather fixed and finds it difficult to adapt or to change his or her mind once it's been made up. Excellent with responsibility. Prefers to work alone. Very strong type.

Note – **whorls come in two types: concentric or spiral. Both carry the same meaning.**

ARCHES

The salt of the earth. Practical, solid, level-headed and down-to-earth. Materialistic. Difficulty in expressing innermost feelings.

TENTED ARCHES

Usually found only on the index or middle fingers. This pattern shows enthusiasm and excitement. Impulsive. Deep involvement in whatever is undertaken.

COMPOSITES

Ability to see both sides of the story. Tendency to overthink when having to make a decision and consequently leading to confusion. Excellent at making judgements for others but finds it difficult to make decisions for self.

PEACOCK'S EYE

Traditionally a lucky omen. Those who possess it, it is said, are blessed with a sense of protection or preservation which seems to save them from danger even at the eleventh hour.

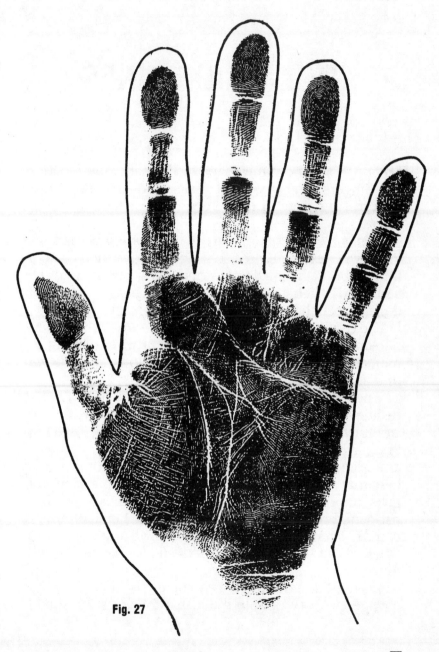

Fig. 27

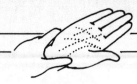

THE MAJOR LINES

Having worked out the shape of the hand, the length of the fingers, the types of nails and the fingerprint patterns, it's now time to focus your attention on the lines.

This is a very exciting part of the reading because the lines will tell you precisely about how their owners think, about the quality of their lives, about how they feel (and when they felt it!) and perhaps more about their career than even they know themselves.

There are four major lines. The *life line* tells about a person's health and well-being, the *head line* about the mentality, the *heart line* about emotions and the *fate line* about one's career or public life.

When you're looking at each line you first have to decide which way it's lying in the palm and then more carefully zoom in on it to see how it's actually made up. You have to ask yourself if it's broken anywhere, if it has any islands in it, and you have to look for branches or bars that might lie across it. Each of these markings will give important information about events that have happened to that person during his or her life. And, of course, even more importantly, it will give you some clues about events that are *likely* to happen in the future.

One thing you must remember is that lines can change. A lot of people think that they're stuck for life

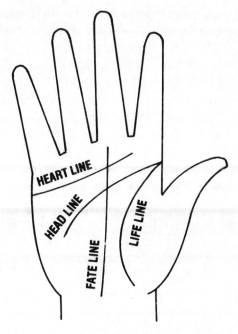

with the lines they're born with. But I wonder if you've ever caught yourself, absent-mindedly perhaps, staring into your palm and suddenly thinking to yourself, 'Oh, I've not seen that line there before!' And then, just as quickly putting it out of your mind with the thought that it must have been there all along but you simply hadn't noticed it before. It's far more likely, though, that you were right first time, that you hadn't spotted it before because it simply wasn't there before.

Lines do have a habit of coming and going, of growing and fading away. The major lines are less likely to do so, of course, although the ends can extend or shrink back according to different circumstances. The state of your health, your life style, the decisions you take or your general attitude to life can all help to shape and change the lines in your hands.

Although it's fairly easy to see which are the head and heart lines, people do sometimes get a little confused over the life line and positively perplexed when it comes to the line of fate. This is, of course, because each hand is so unique that no book on hand reading can ever hope to cover every single pattern of lines in the universe. The best that can be done is that each line is carefully explained and by the time you've worked out your own hands and those of each member of your family and friends you should, hopefully, have had enough practice to recognize a fate line at twenty paces!

THE LIFE LINE

KEY WORDS: **THE QUALITY OF LIFE. HEALTH**

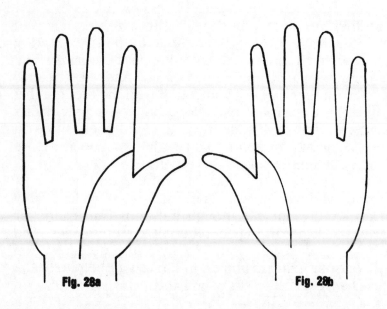

Fig. 28a   Fig. 28b

POSITION	The life line is found skirting around the thumb.
DIRECTION	It is read from the top of the thumb, round and downwards.
MEANING	The life line tells you about the quality of your life. If it's formed into a good wide arc reaching towards the centre of the palm it shows a healthy life and a healthy, well-balanced attitude to life. These people are strong, robust and sexually virile. They have a happy-go-lucky spirit and a love of life. (Fig. **28a**). Tightly skirting the thumb shows a mean, selfish attitude. These people are rather cold and stand-offish. Health-wise they are not particularly robust. (Fig. **28b**).

★ The life line does not indicate how long you are going to live or when you are going to die. A short life line isn't necessarily a sign of a short life. It may suggest a turning point or a new beginning at that moment in life. Equally, a long life line does not necessarily guarantee a long life. What is important in this line is the *quality* of the line which reflects the *quality* of the life that is led.

BEGINNING	Beginning attached to the head line shows a careful, cautious nature. (Fig. **29a**). Separated from it suggests someone who tends to take

risks in life. This is also the sign of an independent spirit. (Fig. **29b**).

ENDING

The life line should sweep around the mount of Venus and end tucked underneath the ball of the thumb at the wrist. Ending any shorter does not imply an early death. More likely, it suggests a big change, such as a move or emigration to another country, for example.

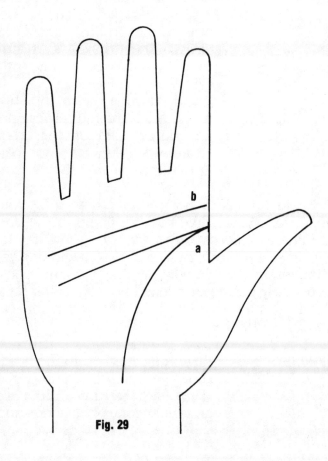

Fig. 29

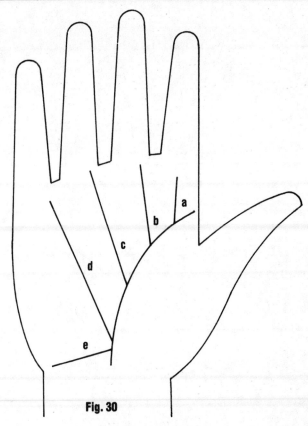

Fig. 30

BRANCHES

Rising branches are a sign of personal achievement. To Jupiter. (Fig. **30a**) shows academic success, to Saturn (Fig. **30b**) suggests buying a new house, to Apollo (Fig. **30c**) tells of happiness due to some form of creative expression and to Mercury (Fig. **30d**) can mean money coming your way.

Branches which drop downwards (Fig. **30e**) usually show movement of some kind, either a change of address or an important journey or holiday.

79

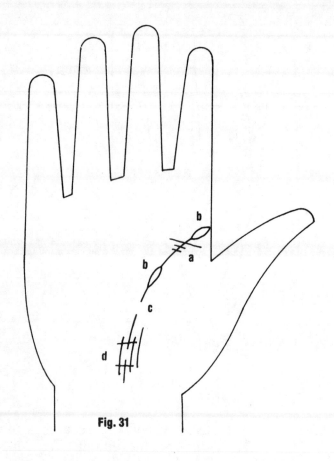

Fig. 31

BARS

Lines that cut right across the life line (Fig. **31a**) are known as bar lines and usually show an emotional upset of some sort. Most people have a few of these lines – some more, some less. Some bars may represent huge emotional upheavals while others stand for minor rows and upsets. If you know you have some of these coming up in the future, it is possible in many cases to prevent the upset from happening and in doing so the bar line can disappear completely.

ISLANDS

Islands (Fig. **31b**) at the beginning of the line show a tendency to bronchial problems and/or early childhood illnesses. In the centre of the line an island suggests back or spinal problems.

Elsewhere, an island in the life line points to physical weakness, illness or simply a strain on the body's reserves.

BREAKS

A break in the line (Fig. **31c**) could show an injury or possibly a change in the way of life. Protection in either case may be represented by something like a square formation over the break or a short parallel line spanning over the break either inside or outside the main line of life. (Fig. **31d**).

THE HEAD LINE

KEY WORDS: **THE HEAD. THE MIND. MEN-TALITY.**

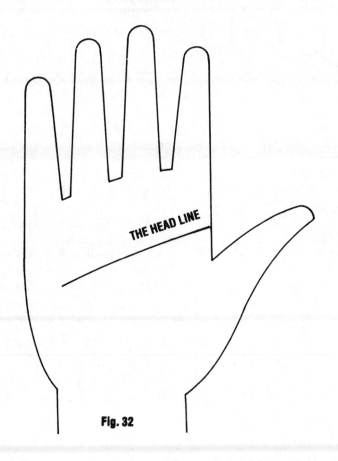

THE HEAD LINE

Fig. 32

POSITION   The head line lies across the palm. If you start from the base of the fingers and work your way down, it is the second horizontal line you reach in the palm. Some head lines are straight and level, some are curved and still others slope steeply towards the wrist.

DIRECTION   The head line is read from its beginning on the thumb side to its end on the opposite side of the palm.

MEANING   The head line deals firstly with the physical head and secondly with the way you think, with your mind and your mentality.

If your line is straight (Fig. **33**) you are practical, logical and materialistic. You tend to think in fairly straight lines. You have a good amount of common sense and are down-to-earth in the way you think. Depending on

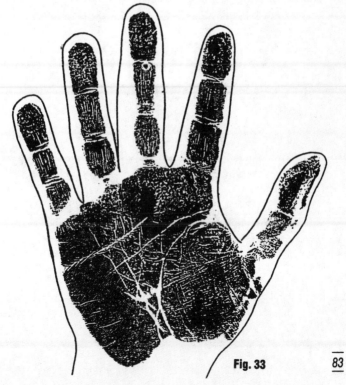

Fig. 33

how academic you are, your interests could include: business, finance, maths, science, technology and all sorts of practical subjects on an 'earthy nature'.

If you head line is curved (Fig. **34**), you have a creative turn of mind. Anything to do with languages, the media, dealing with people would suit you. You would equally enjoy any subjects that come under the heading of Arts – anything of a creative or artistic nature.

If your head line slopes very steeply down towards the opposite bottom corner of the palm you tend to be

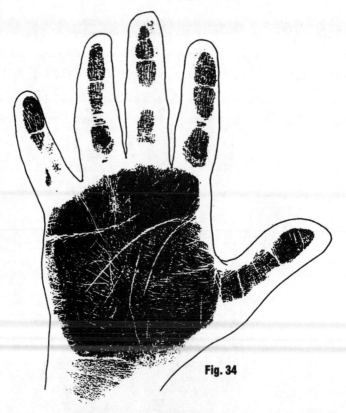

Fig. 34

over-imaginative to the point where your imagination can run away with you unless you take firm control. This can also show melancholia and mood swings. Excellent line for outstanding artistic work – either painting or fiction writing – but those moods must be controlled.

★ There is an unusual form of head line which is known as the 'Simian Line' (see Fig. **35**). This is a thick line that runs right across the middle of the palm almost as if it cuts the hand in two. There is no other horizontal line above it because both the head and heart lines are combined together to form this

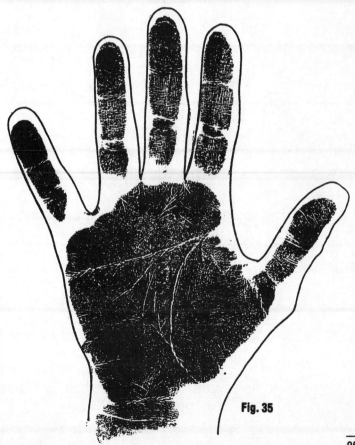

Fig. 35

line. If you possess a Simian Line you might be described as intense because you have a habit of concentrating all your efforts and energies into whatever you are doing at the time. You work hard, you play hard and you love hard. And talking of love – beware of jealousy – at least for the first half of your life. Once past 35, though, your emotions start to mellow.

Fig. 36

BEGINNINGS

If your line begins attached to the life line you are rather cautious and careful. (Fig. **36**). Attached for a long way shows that you were close to your parents and early family life and that you didn't break free into your own independence of mind until a little later than is usual in our modern day.

Fig. 37

Is your line separated as in the illustration? This reveals independence from an early age. The wider the separation the more wilful the personality. A very wide gap shows someone who likes to take risks, who jumps in at the deep end without first having worked out the full implications of his or her actions. (Fig. 37).

ENDINGS

A very short head line ending below the middle finger would show a concrete and materialist attitude to life.

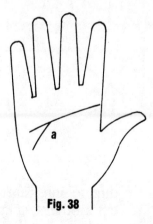

Fig. 38

Fig. 38

If the line is forked beneath the ring finger it is known as the 'writer's fork' and reveals masses of creative talent in the fields of art and literature. (Fig. **38a**).

Another form can occur at the end of the line, this time beneath the little finger. This shows a good head for business and if you have this marking you could do very well in a business of your own. (Fig. **38b**).

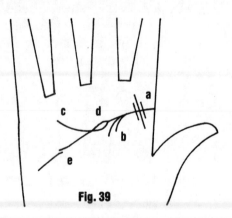

Fig. 39

BARS

Little bar lines cutting across the head line warn of worries mainly due to interference or obstruction from others. (Fig. **39a**).

BRANCHES

Tiny branches that drop down from the head line show particular times of depression. (Fig. **39b**). Branches that rise upwards (Fig. **39c**) are signs of achievement. When a branch rises to the Jupiter mount this is a sign of an academic success. To Saturn would have something to do with property. To Apollo shows happiness, self-fulfilment or a creative achievement of some sort. Towards Mercury tells of business or scientific success or alternatively of financial rewards.

ISLANDS

Islands in the head line reveal times of worry and anxiety. If you have an island in the middle of your line beneath the Saturn finger it suggests that you cannot take stress. (Fig. **39d**). Either avoid stressful situations as much as possible or alternatively learn to recognize and deal with the symptoms.

BREAKS

A break in this line may show a massive change of attitude, a new way of thinking, a different way of looking at life than before. (Fig. **39e**).

THE HEART LINE

KEY WORDS: **LOVE. EMOTIONS. FEELINGS.
RELATIONSHIPS.**

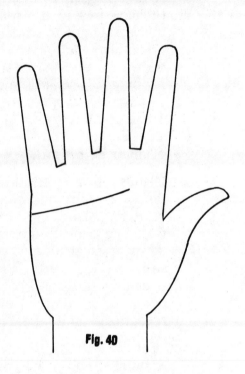

Fig. 40

POSITION

Working down from the fingers the heart line is the first horizontal line lying across the top of the palm.

DIRECTION

The heart line is read from the outer edge of the palm towards the index finger.

MEANING

The heart line, as its name implies, deals with the physical heart and also with your emotions, with your innermost feelings, with your attitudes to love and with the way you relate to other people.

BEGINNING

This line usually begins with a few branches like roots that lead into the main line itself.

ENDING

There are several different endings to this line.

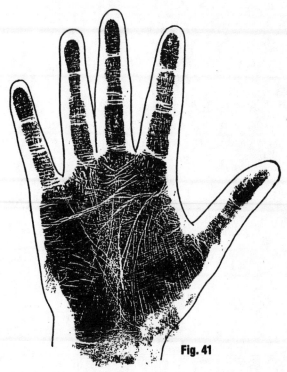

Fig. 41

If your line ends right in the centre of the Jupiter Mount it shows you're very idealistic and romantic and perhaps a little naive when it comes to love and relationships. (Fig. **41**).

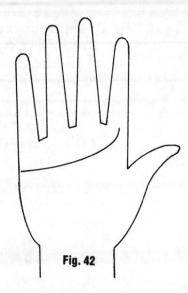

Fig. 42

If you have a line that reaches right up through the mount and touches the base of the index finger it shows that you have high expectations and even higher standards.

Fig. 43

A line that travels straight across the mount almost hitting the edge of the palm shows that work is very important and comes first even above love, marriage and relationships. (Fig. **43**).

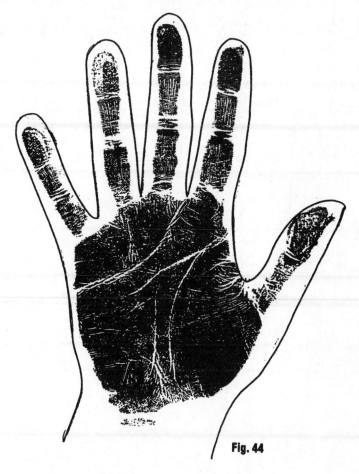

Fig. 44

Does your line sweep right up to end between the first and second fingers as in the illustration? This shows you have lots of common sense in your relationships with others. The only problem with this line is that it shows you tend not to talk about your innermost feelings. Instead, you bottle up your emotions which isn't all that healthy and you should try to find a way of letting them out, either through talking about them with a good friend or perhaps writing it all down in a diary. (Fig. 44).

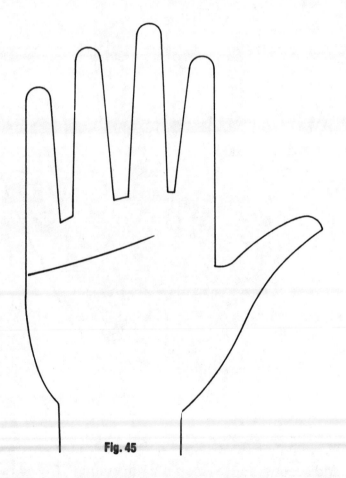

Fig. 45

A short line that ends on the Mount of Saturn is a tell-tale hint of the gigolo type. (Fig. **45**). These people can't seem able to commit themselves to one person, preferring the short-term thrills of a brief affair. If your new boyfriend has this marking beware! He may proverbially be 'only after one thing'.

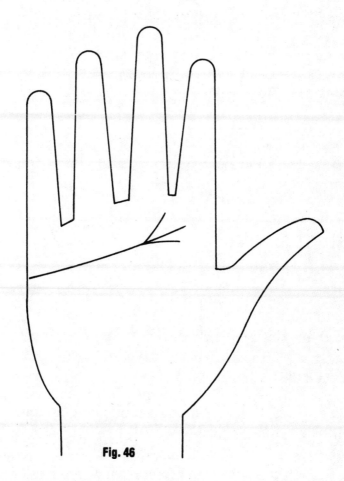

Fig. 46

The best type of heart line to have is one which ends with a fork or, even better, with a trident. This shows a kind, sympathetic, understanding nature. If your partner has one of these you're very lucky indeed as he or she is a deeply loving person and you're likely to have a happy life together. (Fig. **46**).

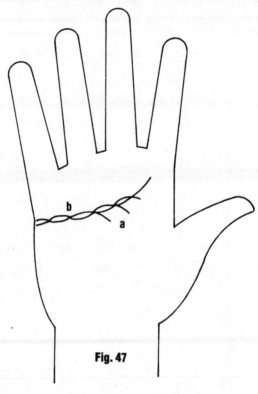

Fig. 47

BRANCHES

Branches that shoot downwards from the heart line show disappointments and emotional upsets. (Fig. **47a**).

ISLANDS

Islands in the heart line often refer to health matters. A series of islands, also known as a chain, can indicate that the body chemistry is out of balance. (Fig. **47b**).

An island in the line beneath the middle finger can sometimes suggest a family history of hearing problems. (Fig. **48a**). And beneath the ring finger, an island in the line can point to problems with sight or with the eyes in general. (Fig. **48b**).

BREAKS

Breaks in the heart line may show physical defects of the heart or that the person is susceptible to illnesses associated with the heart or with the circulation. (Fig. **48c**). This, however, would need to be confirmed by other features elsewhere in the hand.

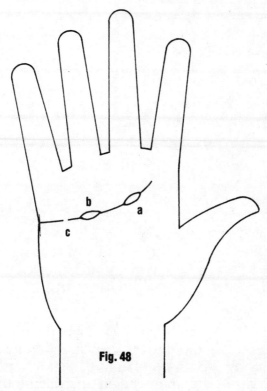

Fig. 48

THE FATE LINE

KEY WORDS: **CAREER. PUBLIC LIFE. SOCIAL LIFE.**

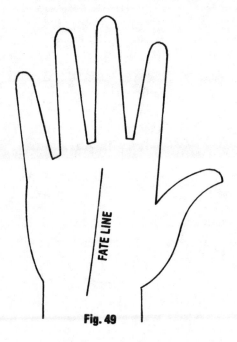

Fig. 49

POSITION   The fate line can sometimes be difficult to find. In some hands it comes in short lengths, it may be broken, it can start half-way up the palm and in other cases it may not even exist at all.

A pure fate line, which is rare to find, starts in the centre of the palm at the wrist, runs upwards in a straight line and ends on the mount beneath the middle finger. Some, however, stem from the life line and shoot upwards whilst others begin on the Mount of Luna.

However it occurs, its position is towards the centre of the palm.

DIRECTION This line is read from the wrist upwards towards the fingers.

MEANING The fate line deals with your career, your public and social way of life. It shows your feelings of material success and your ideas about your social standing in life. It tells about your job, working colleagues and your financial situation. Any changes in your way of life, whether public or social, is recorded in this line.

If you don't have one of these lines, don't worry, it simply means that you're not hampered or restricted by a need to conform to standards or pressures that are set up by society.

BEGINNING The fate line can stem from several different places in the palm.

The normal beginning for this line is close to the centre of the top bracelet on the wrist and shooting straight up the middle of the palm to the Saturn finger. (Fig. **50a**). If you have this line you're the sort of person who follows a set path in life.

If your line begins on the Luna Mount you need to work with people. Well-known celebrities and those who work in the public eye often have this fate line. (Fig. **50b**).

When the line begins attached to the life line it shows early responsibilities and family commitments – the sort of situation, let's say, when a young boy has to take on

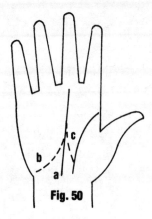

Fig. 50

the mantle of responsibility and become the 'man of the house' due to his father's ill-health or early death. (Fig. **50c**).

If the line doesn't start at the bottom of the hand but appears some way up it shows a lack of direction in life during the early years. A sense of purpose and a settling down occurs at the point when the fate line begins. (Fig. **51a**).

ENDING   The usual ending for the fate line is on the Saturn mount. This shows a steady, settled life. (Fig. **51b**).

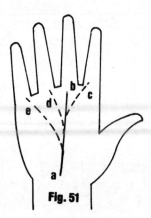

Fig. 51

If your line swerves and ends below the index it's a sign that you could reach a position of power and influence in your work and life. Famous people often have a fate line that begins on Luna and ends on Jupiter. (Fig. **51c**).

Ending on Apollo shows a life of personal contentment and success, often associated with literature or the Arts. (Fig. **51d**).

When the line swerves the other way and ends beneath the little finger it augurs wealth and success in business or scientific work. (Fig. **51e**).

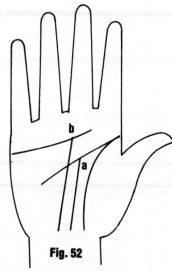

Fig. 52

Sometimes the line comes to an abrupt end as it reaches the head line. This is not a good sign as it suggests a severe set-back to the person's career due to some sort of misjudgement or bad management in his or her work. (Fig. **52a**).

If the line should suddenly stop on the heart line it suggests that the life and career suffer due to emotional problems and complications. (Fig. **52b**).

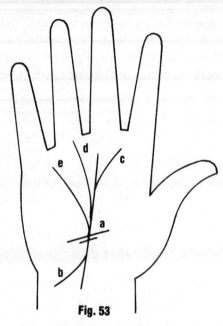

Fig. 53

BARS

Any short bar crossing the fate line warns of interference or obstruction in the course of that person's life or career. (Fig. **53a**).

BRANCHES

Branches from the Luna Mount running to join the fate line are signs of relationships or marriage. (Fig. **53b**).

Other branches that rise upwards towards the fingers are good signs. To Jupiter shows general success in the career. A branch to Apollo could well indicate fame (Fig. **53c**). And one to Mercury suggests untold wealth (Fig. **53e**).

ISLANDS

Islands in the lines are not good signs as they warn of frustration and dissatisfaction either at work or life in general. An island can also show a period of financial worries when money could be tight (Fig. **54a**).

BREAKS

Breaks in this line always denote changes either of jobs and career or of life-style. A clean break in the line tells of a change that is forced upon the owner, perhaps suddenly being made redundant or forcefully evicted from a much-loved house. (Fig. **54b**).

But a break in the line which is overlapped by a new section of fate line is quite different. (Fig. **54c**). If you have one of these it shows that you have chosen to make the change. Perhaps it tells of a promotion, a new job, a change of address. The bigger the gap between the overlapped sections of line, the bigger the change you have decided to make.

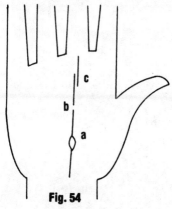

Fig. 54

THE SECONDARY LINES

At some point or other you may come across a hand that has only the few lines of life, head and heart. At the other extreme you may find someone whose hand is so covered with lines it looks as if a spider has spun a cobweb into the palm.

The lines that make up some of that 'spider web' are known as secondary or minor lines. These include the Apollo line, the Mercury line, the Girdle of Venus, the Via Lascivia and the Bow of Intuition. Just as with the major lines these, too, can change, can grow or fade according to your circumstances.

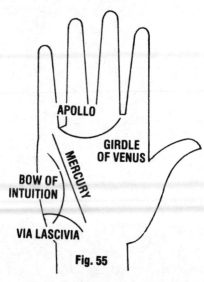

Fig. 55

THE LINE OF APOLLO

KEY WORDS: **CREATIVITY. SUCCESS. FAME. HAPPINESS.**

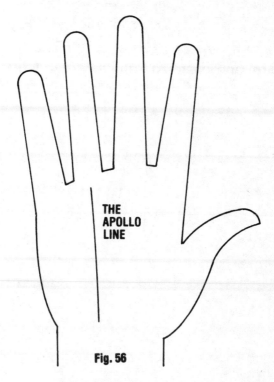

THE APOLLO LINE

Fig. 56

POSITION

The Apollo line runs upwards and ends on the mount beneath the ring finger. Sometimes it runs parallel to the fate line, sometimes it shoots out of the fate line itself. In many hands it exists only above the heart line and in a few hands it begins right down at the wrist.

MEANING — This line tells of creative expression and a deep sense of contentment in life. It is a lucky line to possess as it augurs success and, in some cases, fame.

BEGINNING — The Apollo line can start from several different points in the palm.

If your line starts above the heart line you can be sure of a warm and contented old age. (Fig. **57a**).

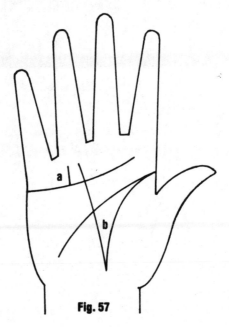

Fig. 57

Branching out from the fate line shows success and contentment from the time at which the Apollo line leaves the main fate line. (Fig. **57b**).

When the line begins in the centre of the palm, as in the hand print illustrated (see Fig. **58**), it shows that success will come from personal effort usually after thirty.

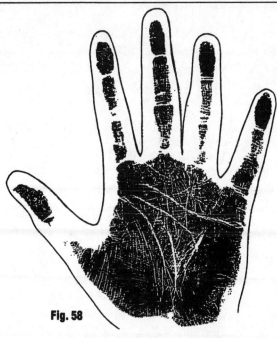

Fig. 58

Hard work and personal effort will bring success if you have an Apollo line that sweeps in from the outer edge of the palm. (Fig. **59a**).

A very rare form of the line is seen when it begins low down in the hand and rises straight up to the Apollo Mount. (Fig. **59b**). If any of your young children have this marking start collecting all their bits of drawings and writings because one day you could make a fortune

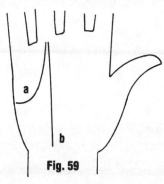

Fig. 59

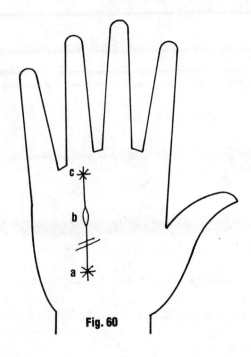

Fig. 60

selling them to the Sunday papers! You see, this extraordinary line is the mark of fame and points to a brilliant career.

MARKINGS   Crosses or bars on the line suggest
                            obstacles, set-backs and opposition.
                            (Fig. **60a**).

An island warns that you should guard against scandal, a loss of reputation or a bad press in your life or career. (Fig. **60b**).

A star, though, is a wonderful omen of brilliance and success. (Fig. **60c**).

THE MERCURY LINE

KEY WORDS: **HEALTH. DIGESTION. BUSINESS.**

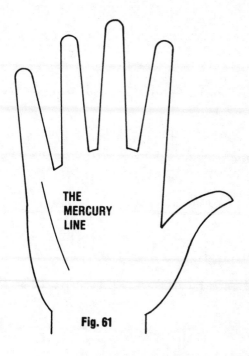

THE
MERCURY
LINE

Fig. 61

POSITION

The Mercury line can begin in several different places in the palm. It may start from the Mount of Venus, across the life line, it may come from the base of the hand or it may be missing altogether. When present, it travels up the palm and ends beneath the little finger.

MEANING This line covers two quite different areas. Firstly, it tells us about our health and secondly it reveals our ability or sense for business.

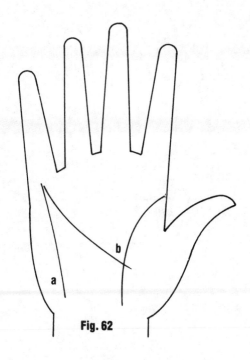

Fig. 62

BEGINNING Ideally, this line should start at the base of the palm on the Mount of Luna and rise in a straight line up to the Mount of Mercury. (Fig. **62a**). This sort of line tells of good health. It also shows a good, clear head for business and success in the field of commerce.

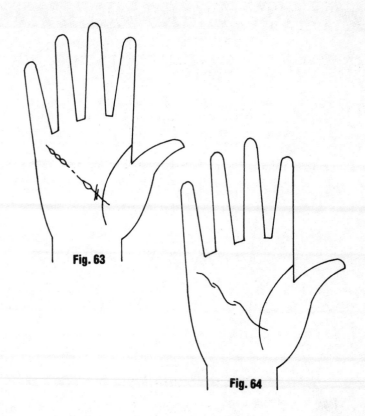

Fig. 63

Fig. 64

Starting from the life line or the Mount of Venus, the Mercury line tells of poor digestion, of acidity and a tendency to suffer from nervous tension. (Fig. **62b**).

Healthwise, it is better if the line doesn't exist at all.

MARKINGS   Any breaks, chains, islands or bars that cut through the line suggest periods of ill-health and/or worries and anxieties about work or business. (Fig. **63**).

A wavy, twisting line tells of digestive troubles. (Fig. **64**).

111

THE GIRDLE OF VENUS

KEY WORDS: **SENSUALITY. SEXINESS. SENSI-TIVITY.**

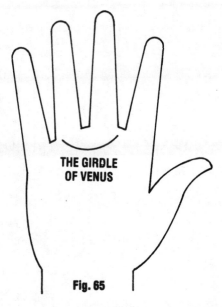

THE GIRDLE
OF VENUS

Fig. 65

POSITION   The Girdle of Venus is a semi-circular line which is found above the heart line curving around the base of the two middle fingers.

MEANING   This line is not often found in its complete form. When it is it shows an out-and-out sensual nature, possibly even verging on depravity.

It is best when made up of several strands. Like this, the line tells of a sensitive but lively person, someone who seems to have a magnetic appeal to others or what is known as 'charisma'.

Fig. 66

In some hands, when it is made up of tiny sections or when only fragments of the semi-circle are seen, it can suggest a highly sensitive, highly strung and nervous person. (Fig. **66**).

THE VIA LASCIVIA

KEY WORDS: **ALLERGY. PHYSICAL SENSI-TIVITIES.**

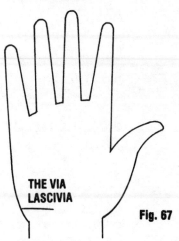

**THE VIA
LASCIVIA**

Fig. 67

POSITION   The Via Lascivia is found at the base of the palm lying across the Mount of Luna.

MEANING

This line is now more commonly known as the 'Allergy' line because when it occurs in a hand it reveals a sensitivity to certain foods. If you have this line watch your diet carefully to see if you have any symptoms or reactions to certain food-stuffs. If you're perpetually overweight despite the agonies of dieting, check to see if you have this line. If you have, it could well be that this is the way your body is telling you that it is intolerant to certain foods. Perhaps by finding out what you are allergic to and cutting that out of your diet, you might solve your weight problem forever.

THE BOW OF INTUITION

KEY WORDS:

PSYCHIC POWER. PRECOGNITION.

POSITION

As its name suggests this line takes the form of a bow which stands upright, facing the edge of the palm, starting on the Mount of Luna and ending beneath the little finger.

MEANING

If you have this line you are blessed with plenty of intuition. You're the sort who tends to have prophetic

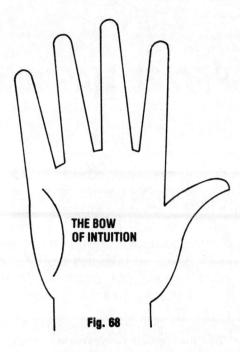

**THE BOW
OF INTUITION**

Fig. 68

dreams and you seem to have an uncanny knack of knowing something's going to happen before it actually does. Clairvoyants, people with telepathic powers or with a highly developed sixth sense have this marking. If you have it too, listen to that inner voice and let your natural intuition guide you through life.

SPECIAL MARKINGS

When you start to examine your hands closely and those of the other members of your family, you're likely to come across a variety of markings made up of little lines. Not all hands will have these marks. Some may have one or two, some will have lots of them and others possibly none at all. They're fun to hunt for and some will give pretty strong pointers to hidden talents and even the sort of careers to go for.

THE TEACHER'S SQUARE

Fig. 69

POSITION   Four short lines formed into the shape of a square lying on the Jupiter Mount beneath the index finger.

MEANING   As its name implies this marking shows a special talent for teaching and a natural gift for passing on information.

THE MEDICAL STIGMATA

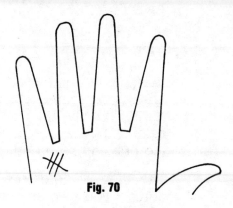

Fig. 70

POSITION   Three short vertical lines, often with a horizontal one across them so that it looks like an old-fashioned TV aerial. This marking is found directly beneath the inside edge of the little finger.

MEANING   The Medical Stigmata is a very special mark as it shows natural healing powers. Doctors, nurses, vets, psychologists, counsellors, healers of all types often have this formation.

117

THE RING OF SOLOMON

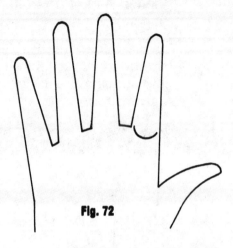

Fig. 72

POSITION

This is a semi-circular line that starts from the thumb edge of the palm and sweeps up to end between the first and second fingers.

MEANING

The Ring of Solomon shows wisdom. If you have this marking you are a wise person with a great deal of understanding which would stand you in good stead in any job dealing directly with people.

THE RING OF SATURN

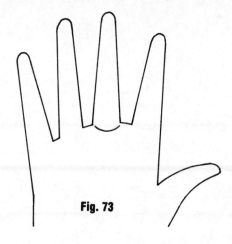

Fig. 73

POSITION

The Ring of Saturn is a curved line that looks rather like a collar around the base of the middle finger. It begins between the first and second fingers and sweeps round to end between the second and third fingers.

MEANING

This is a rather negative marking for it shows a gloomy, jaundiced view of life. If you have this mark you're likely to be forever expecting the worse to happen and because you do you will attract negative things like a magnet. You can, however, make this line disappear by changing your attitude and looking on the bright side of life!

RELATIONSHIP LINES

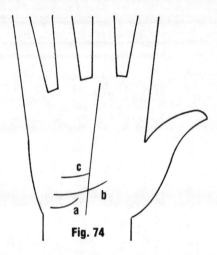

Fig. 74

POSITION

These lines take the form of sloping branches which begin on the Mount of Luna and run up to meet the fate line.

MEANING

The branches are known as influence, or relationship lines and the times at which the relationship is struck up, whether the couple marry or split up can all be measured against the fate line.

If a branch reaches up towards the fate line but doesn't quite meet it, it tells that the relationship won't come to anything (Fig. **74a**).

When the branch does reach the fate line but crosses right over it's perhaps even worse than if the line fails to meet. In this case it shows that the relationship is called off at the very last minute, just as the wedding invitations are being sent out, so to speak (Fig. **74b**).

But, when the branch reaches up to meet and merges into the fate line it is a classical sign of marriage, or at least of setting up home together (Fig. **74c**).

CHILDREN LINES

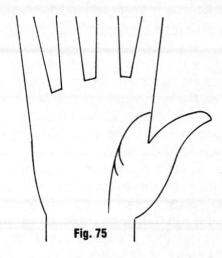

Fig. 75

POSITION	Children lines can be found as tiny branches that sweep out from inside of the life line.
MEANING	These tiny branches are also signs of responsibilities. At the top half of the line they can suggest children but further down they may refer to other new responsibilities coming into the home, such as a special foster child, perhaps, or granny moving in with the family.

TIME

Do you ever wish you could see into the future? Or wish that with hindsight you hadn't moved, got married, changed jobs, or whatever? Having read through this book you should by now have picked up lots of information about yourself, your family, your loved ones, your friends and acquaintances. When you look at your hands you will be able to spot trends, detect things that have happened and see possible events that are likely to happen in the future.

But in order to get a clear picture you will have to be able to date and time the events you see. This can be a little tricky on hands because unfortunately they don't all come in uniform shapes and sizes. Some are big, some are small. Some are narrow, some are wide.

Nevertheless, there is a system which should give you a fairly good idea but you will have to slightly stretch it or compress it according to the size of the hand. Some people find that measurements are more easily taken on a print than on the actual hand. Whichever, the more you do, of course, the easier it gets.

Time is successfully measured only on the three main lines of life, head and fate.

TIME ON THE LIFE LINE

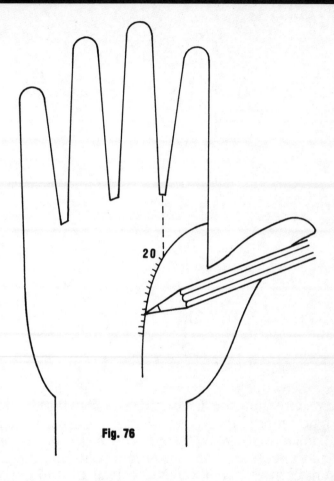

Fig. 76

If you draw a straight line down from the inside edge of the index finger it should strike the life line at about 20 years of age. With the sharp point of a pencil you count in years forwards and backwards from that mark. One year is roughly the same width as the pencil point. Make it slightly longer for a very large hand, slightly narrower for a very small hand.

THE HEAD LINE

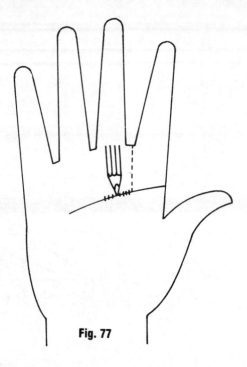

Fig. 77

Using exactly the same system as on the life line, draw a straight line from the inside edge of the index finger down to reach the head line. This point marks approximately 20 years of age. The head line is read from the thumb side out across the palm and you can measure each year backwards or forwards from this 20-year mark by using a sharp-pointed pencil. Starting at the 20-year mark, move the pencil point about 1 mm forward each time you want to add on one year, or back from the 20-year mark to subtract one year. Just to confirm your accuracy, you should find that 13 lies directly beneath the centre of the index finger and 35 beneath the centre of the middle one.

THE FATE LINE

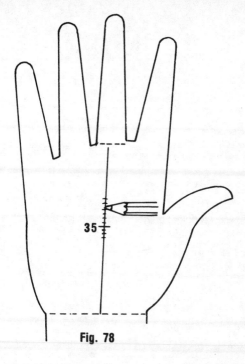

Fig. 78

The fate line is read from the base of the hand upwards towards the fingers. This line can be a little tricky to time because it doesn't always run in a conveniently straight line. It does get easier, though, with practice. So to time this line, you must draw a vertical line from the base of the middle finger to the top bracelet at the wrist. Measure this line and divide it in half. Mark the halfway point as 35 years. Then, with the point of your pencil, you can mark off the years, one for each mm, added on *above* the 35-year mark up towards the fingers and subtracted from below the mark towards the wrist. To transfer these times on to the fate line, simply slide your pencil across from the vertical line on to the main fate line itself.

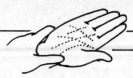

INDEX